COOL
Exercise

HEALTHY & FUN WAYS TO GET YOUR BODY MOVING

Colleen Dolphin

A Division of ABDO

ABDO
Publishing Company

visit us at www.abdopublishing.com

Published by ABDO Publishing Company, a division of ABDO, P.O. Box 398166, Minneapolis, Minnesota 55439. Copyright © 2013 by Abdo Consulting Group, Inc. International copyrights reserved in all countries. No part of this book may be reproduced in any form without written permission from the publisher. Checkerboard Library™ is a trademark and logo of ABDO Publishing Company.

Printed in the United States of America, North Mankato, Minnesota
062012
092012

 PRINTED ON RECYCLED PAPER

Design and Production: Mighty Media, Inc.
Series Editor: Liz Salzmann
Photo Credits: Colleen Dolphin, Shutterstock

The following manufacturers/names appearing in this book are trademarks: Crayola®, Sharpie®, Sportline®

Library of Congress Cataloging-in-Publication Data

Dolphin, Colleen, 1979-
 Cool exercise : healthy & fun ways to get your body moving / Colleen Dolphin.
     p. cm. -- (Cool health & fitness)
 Includes index.
 ISBN 978-1-61783-427-1
 1. Exercise for children--Juvenile literature. I. Title.
 GV443.D64 2012
 613.7'042--dc23
                              2012010053

CONTENTS

WORK IT OUT!

It's time to get up and find your groove! Exercise is a great way to stay healthy and be you. Exercise also **boosts** your brainpower and gives you more energy. This book will show you how.

There are a lot of ways to have fun keeping fit. Are you a soccer player or a swimmer? Maybe you like to ride your bicycle or skateboard. Don't be afraid of doing something different! You just might find a new activity you will love. Get started today!

Permission & Safety

- Always get **permission** before doing these activities.
- Always ask if you can use the tools, supplies, or exercise gear you need.
- If you do something by yourself, make sure you do it safely.
- Ask for help when necessary.
- Be careful when using sharp objects.
- Make sure you're wearing the **appropriate** gear.

Be Prepared

- Read the entire activity before you begin.
- Make sure you have all the tools and materials listed.
- Do you have enough time to complete the activity?
- Keep your work area clean and organized.
- Follow the directions.
- Clean up any mess you make.

5

WHY EXERCISE?

Exercise makes you feel good about yourself and how you look. It makes you strong. It can even give you more energy! Plus, it's easy to do. You don't need special equipment to exercise every day. Go for a walk or try doing sit-ups. Whether you are by yourself or with friends, it's fun to be active!

Prevent Injuries!

- Make sure your clothing and protective gear fits properly.

- Warm up before the activity and cool down afterward.

- Follow the rules and use proper exercise **techniques**.

- Do not exercise if you are sick or hurt.

STAY HYDRATED!

The human body is about 60% water. Water helps transport energy through the cells in your body. Active kids like you need at least six glasses of water every day!

WEIGH OF LIFE

The right weight for each person is hard to calculate. Everyone is different. Your genes and **lifestyle** are a big part of your body shape. Your genes affect things like your height, your skeletal frame, and how much muscle you have. Lifestyle is important too. Exercising and eating healthy foods help you stay fit.

As long as you stay active and eat right, you won't need to worry about your weight. That's pretty great. You'll have more time to think about exciting things, like sports and friends!

MAKE TIME TO EXERCISE!

AROUND THE HOUSE (INSIDE)

There's more to do than watch TV when you're inside your house. It's okay to watch TV for a little while. But you should also try to move around and get your heart rate going!

AROUND THE HOUSE (OUTSIDE)

If the weather is nice, why not enjoy the fresh air outside? You won't have to worry about breaking anything when throwing or kicking a ball. And you can run as fast as you want!

ACTIVE VIDEO GAMES

Playing video games doesn't mean using only your hands. Now there are games where you can bowl, dance, or even play different sports!

PLUGGED IN

Computers are used for a lot of things. Most kids use them for talking to friends and doing homework. But it's important to take quick breaks to exercise your muscles. No one likes a stiff neck or back!

ON THE ROAD

Car rides, especially road trips, can seem long. Exercising in the car helps keep your mind and body busy. Before you know it, you'll arrive at your **destination**!

AT SCHOOL

Most of your school day is spent sitting. It's easy to get restless! Exercise helps you stay focused on what you're learning. Try doing something active in between classes.

WITH FRIENDS

You can do so many fun things when you are with your friends. Find activities that you all like to do. Take turns trying each other's favorites.

SUPER MUSCLE STRENGTH!

Having strong muscles is important. It helps you stay healthy. Try strength training. It builds up your muscles with controlled movements. You've probably already done some strength training moves like sit-ups, pull-ups, and push-ups! Other strength training exercises use resistance bands. Strength training is a great way to improve your muscles.

With every exercise you do, first make sure to be safe. Ask for help if you don't know how to do something. And don't push yourself if you feel tired.

WARMING UP AND COOLING DOWN

Warming up and cooling down is important. It will help prevent injuries. Warming up gets your blood flowing to your muscles, getting them ready for exercise! Cooling down gets your muscles and body temperature back to normal.

A warm-up can be as easy as a brisk walk. Warm up for about 15 minutes.

After you finish exercising, make sure to cool down. Try walking slowly for 10 minutes.

STRETCH IT OUT!

Try stretching before exercising but after warming up. Remember these tips:

- Don't **bounce** when stretching.

- Make sure the stretch is gentle. Don't force a stretch until you're in pain.

- Stretch with slow movements so you don't injure yourself.

SUPPLIES

Here are some of the things that you'll need to get started!

black permanent marker

blank sticky labels

computer

flying disc

refrigerator

large plastic hoops

magnetic business cards

markers

medium-size sponge ball

newspaper

paint pens

paper

pencil

printer

stopwatch

Shake, Swing, Lift, and Rotate

Test your hand-eye coordination!

WHAT YOU NEED

- 20 magnetic business cards
- markers
- refrigerator
- a friend

swing   right leg

shake   left foot

lift   right arm

wiggle   left elbow

1. Write a different body part on 10 of the magnetic cards.

2. Write an action verb on each of the other 10 cards. Keep these cards in a separate pile.

3. Lay both piles of cards face down. Mix each pile up.

4. The first player picks one action card and one body card. He or she sticks them next to each other on the refrigerator. Then that player does what the cards say. If the body card says "left arm" and the action card says "shake," the player shakes his or her left arm.

5. The next player picks cards and puts them below the first player's cards. Then he or she tries to do both sets of actions. Alternate actions if it's not possible to do them at the same time.

6. Take turns drawing cards. Each pair of cards should build on the previous actions. Try to do all of the actions. Everyone's a winner in this game that gets you moving!

ACTION VERBS: shake, rotate, swing, lift, **flex**, wiggle, bend

2

4

Soaring Disc Hoops

Watch your disc fly!

WHAT YOU NEED

- paper
- pencil
- flying disc
- black permanent marker
- newspaper
- paint pens
- large plastic hoop

1. First, **customize** your flying disc! Sketch out ideas on paper. Draw your favorite design on the flying disc with a black permanent marker.

2. Cover a table with newspaper. Use paint pens to color in your design! Let it dry.

3. When the disc is dry it's time to play! Find an area outside with a lot of room. Make sure it's not near the street! Set the large plastic hoop on the ground. Move 10 feet (3 m) away. Try to throw the flying disc so it lands in the hoop.

4. If that's too easy, move farther away from the hoop. Keep making it more challenging!

5. Get some friends to play with you. See who can get the flying disc in the hoop from the greatest distance!

TIP: It's okay if you only have a disc with a design already on it. Try painting over the design or adding a fun border. Or just use the disc as it is.

Guess What?

Act out in the car while you exercise!

WHAT YOU NEED

- markers
- blank sticky labels
- a friend or sibling
- stopwatch

18

1. On a blank label, write down an animal. Make sure the person you're playing with does not see what you write!

2. Stick the label on the other person's back. He or she should do the same for you.

3. One player should act out clues to hint at the animal they wrote down. See if the other player can guess it in 3 minutes or less. You'll be sitting down, but try to use as much movement as possible. Be dramatic!

4. When 3 minutes are up, it's the other player's turn to act like the animal he or she wrote down. After those 3 minutes are up, check the labels. See who guessed correctly.

1

ANIMAL IDEAS

cat	kangaroo
chicken	monkey
dog	lion
eagle	elephant
bunny	giraffe

Muscles in Motion

Get fit while you sit in a car!

WHAT YOU NEED

* just you!

Squeeze Your Abs

1 Tighten your abs. These are your stomach muscles. Hold for 30 to 60 seconds. Make sure you keep breathing. Relax. Do this 10 times.

Stretch Your Arms

2 Reach your arms up as far as you can. Lower your arms and shake them. Repeat 10 times.

Roll Your Shoulders

3 Relax your shoulders. Slowly lift and rotate your shoulders forward 10 times. Reverse the rotation and repeat 10 times.

Rotate Your Wrists

4 Rotate your wrists one direction 10 times. Then rotate them in the other direction 10 times.

Flex Your Calves

5 Raise your heels over your toes. Then rest them back down. Repeat 15 times.

Rotate Your Ankles

6 Rotate your ankles one direction 10 times. Then rotate them in the other direction 10 times.

Homework Buddy Break

WHAT YOU NEED

- computer
- Internet access
- e-mail address
- a friend

1. This activity requires planning! Find a friend who will be doing homework at the same time as you. Ask him or her to try this activity with you.

2. Exchange e-mail addresses with your friend. Set up the times for your homework breaks. Try every 45 minutes or hour.

3. Each of you should make a list of challenges for the other person to do during the breaks.

4. Right before you start your homework, e-mail the first challenge to your friend. He or she should e-mail one to you too.

5. When it's time for your break, check your e-mail. See what you need to do. Maybe it's running up and down the stairs at your house five times. You can even time yourself!

6. After you complete the challenge, report back to your friend. Tell him or her how it went. In the same e-mail, send a new challenge for the next study break.

7. Keep e-mailing challenges and reports for as long as you are studying. That way you'll be taking healthy study breaks!

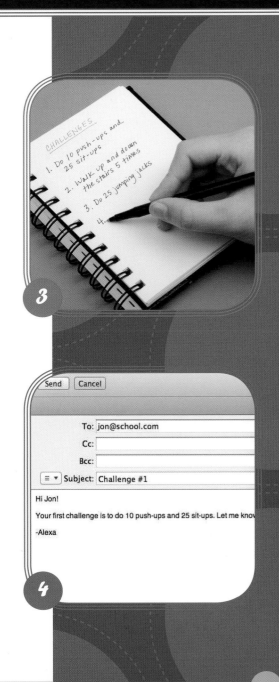

Zip-Lip Ball

Try not to make any noise!

WHAT YOU NEED

- medium-size sponge ball
- classmates

1 Suggest this game to your teacher. Have everyone in the classroom stand up. You can stand in a circle or at your desks. Just do whatever makes sense for the space.

2 One person tosses the ball to another person using an underhand throw. Then that person tosses it to someone else. Keep going until the ball gets thrown to everyone. The ball can't be thrown back to the person who just threw it unless there are only two players left in the game.

3 The trick is that everyone must be completely silent! Anyone who makes a noise is out of the game and must sit down. People who are out still have to stay silent.

4 If a player who is sitting down is able to catch the ball, he or she may re-enter the game. The players sitting down are not allowed to leave their seats to catch the ball. The last person standing is the winner!

YOU'RE OUT!
There are many variations of this game, but some things that can get you out are:
- talking
- whispering
- laughing
- dropping the ball
- throwing the ball too hard

Scavenger Hunt!

No GPS needed to find this treasure!

WHAT YOU NEED

- at least four players
- two unique objects
- paper
- pencil
- computer
- Internet access
- printer
- marker

1. Meet at someone's house. The house is home base. Split into two teams. Each team needs a **unique**, inexpensive object to hide. Make sure each team doesn't know what the other team's object is!

2. Have both teams head outside to hide their objects. Set a time to meet back at home base.

3. Each team should hide their object in a safe place in the neighborhood. Try a park or a neighbor's yard. Make sure to get **permission** first!

4. Each team writes down the address closest to the team's hiding spot.

5. Back at home base, the teams take turns looking up their addresses online. There are several good map Web sites to choose from.

MAP WEB SITES

- Google Maps
  www.google.com/maps
- Yahoo Maps
  www.yahoo.com/maps
- Bing Maps
  www.bing.com/maps
- Mapquest
  www.mapquest.com

TIP:
Make sure to check with an adult before going to hide the object. He or she will know if the area you want to hide your object is safe.

6 **Zoom** in so it shows a few blocks around the hiding spot. Make sure the street names are visible. Each team prints their map.

7 Each team uses an *X* to mark the location of their hidden object on their map.

8 Then each team writes down a few clues about their object. The teams give each other their map and list of clues.

9 Now it's time to hunt for the treasure! Each team leaves at the same time to go looking for the other team's object. The first team back to home base with the object wins!

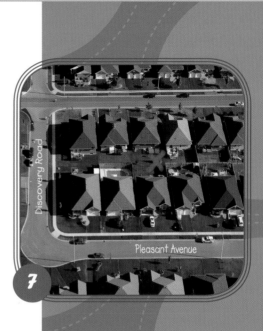

CLUES
1. It is blue.
2. It has eyes
3. It holds money.
4. It

Health Journal

Try keeping a health and fitness journal! Write down any exercises or physical activity you do. Record what you eat too. This makes it easy to look back and see how you are staying healthy and fit. It could also show you where there's room for improvement. Decorate your journal to show your personal style!

Glossary

appropriate – suitable, fitting, or proper for a specific occasion.

boost – to increase or raise.

bounce – to spring up or back after hitting something.

customize – to build, fit, or change something to suit yourself or another person.

destination – the place where you are going to.

flex – to bend and stretch a muscle in the body.

lifestyle – the way a person, group, or society lives.

permission – when a person in charge says it's okay to do something.

technique – a method or style in which something is done.

unique – different, unusual, or special.

zoom – to change the size of an image on a computer screen or camera.

web sites

To learn more about health and fitness for kids, visit ABDO Publishing Company online at www.abdopublishing.com. Web sites about ways for kids to stay fit and healthy are featured on our Book Links page. These links are routinely monitored and updated to provide the most current information available.

Index